DISCARDED

4/9/12

A World of Field Trips

Going to a Farm

Rebecca Rissman

Heinemann Library
Chicago, Illinois

www.capstonepub.com
Visit our website to find out more information about Heinemann-Raintree books.

To order:

☎ Phone 888-454-2279

 Visit www.capstonepub.com to browse our catalog and order online.

© 2012 Heinemann Library
an imprint of Capstone Global Library, LLC
Chicago, Illinois

Edited by Rebecca Rissman, Dan Nunn, and Catherine Veitch
Designed by Richard Parker
Picture research by Tracy Cummins
Originated by Capstone Global Library Ltd
Printed and bound in China by Leo Paper Products Ltd

15 14 13 12 11
10 9 8 7 6 5 4 3 2 1

Library of Congress Cataloging-in-Publication Data
Rissman, Rebecca.
  Going to a farm / Rebecca Rissman.—1st ed.
    p. cm.—(A world of field trips)
  Includes bibliographical references and index.
  ISBN 978-1-4329-6066-7 (hb)—ISBN 978-1-4329-6075-9 (pb)
1. Farms—Juvenile literature. 2. School field trips—Juvenile literature. 3. Agriculture—Juvenile literature. I. Title.
  S519.R56 2012
  630—dc23   2011015149

Acknowledgments
We would like to thank the following for permission to reproduce photographs: Corbis pp. 13 (© John Gress), 21 (© moodboard); Getty Images pp. 5 (Sam Bloomberg-Rissman), 8 (Andy Sacks), 17 (Aldo Sessa), 20 (Judith Haeusler); istockphoto p. 19 (© AVTG); Photolibrary pp. 6 (Peter Frank), pp. 15, 23d (Juice Images); Shutterstock pp. 4 (© Tatiana Sayig), 7, (© Shestakoff), 9 (© shupian), 10 (© Worldpics), 11 (© Muellek Josef), 12 (© Lijuan Guo), 14 (© Sebastian Knight), 16 (© G. Campbell), 18 (© Rich Koele), 22 (© Alexander Gitlits), 23a (© Lijuan Guo), 23b (© G. Campbell), 23c (© Worldpics).

Front cover photograph of a farmer reproduced with permission of Shutterstock (© photofriday). Back cover photograph of a farmer on a rice farm reproduced with permission of Shutterstock (© Worldpics).

Every effort has been made to contact copyright holders of any material reproduced in this book. Any omissions will be rectified in subsequent printings if notice is given to the publisher.

Contents

Field Trips

People take field trips to visit
new places.

People take field trips to learn
new things.

Field Trip to a Farm

Some people take field trips
to farms.

They find out how farms work.

Some farms grow plants.

Some farms raise animals. Some farms do both!

Different Farms

This is a rice farm.

You can see rice growing in
rice paddies.

This is a cranberry farm.

You can see cranberries floating
in bogs.

This is a sheep farm.

You can see farmers shearing sheep.

This is a dairy farm.

You can see cows being milked.

This is a corn farm.

You can see tractors in the fields.

How Should You Act at a Farm?

Remember to listen to the adults.

Don't touch the animals or tools unless an adult tells you that it is okay.

What Do You Think?

What kind of farm is this?

Look on page 24 for the answer.

Picture Glossary

 **bog** area of land that is very wet

 **farm** area of land used for growing crops or raising animals

 **rice paddy** field where rice is grown. Rice paddies are usually flooded with water.

 **shear** cut the wool off sheep

Index

Notes to Parents and Teachers

Before reading
Explain to children that a field trip is a short visit to a new place, and that it often takes place during a school day. Ask children if they have ever taken a field trip. Explain to children that farms are places where animals and plants are raised. Encourage children to think of different types of farms and make a list of their suggestions on the board.

After reading
- Ask children to write down what they ate for breakfast. Then stimulate a group discussion about what types of farms their breakfast foods came from. For example: their banana came from a banana farm, and their milk came from a dairy farm.

Answer to page 22
It is a tulip farm.